Somewhere In Between

Somewhere In Between

By Virginia Archer

Virginia Archer Publishing
2016

Copyright © 2016 by Jean Mederick

All rights reserved. This book or any portion thereof may not be reproduced or used in any manner whatsoever without the express written permission of the publisher except for the use of brief quotations in a book review or scholarly journal.

First Printing: 2016

ISBN 978-976-96004-0-9

Virginia Archer Publishing
P.O. Box 954
Castries, LC04 101
Saint Lucia
http://virginia-archer.tumblr.com/

Front cover art by Nicole Edgecombe "Pure Love" ©
nedgecombeart@gmail.com

Back cover art by Jean Mederick "Kindred" ©
http://virginia-archer.simplesite.com/

Ordering Information:
Special discounts are available on quantity purchases by corporations, associations, educators, and others. For details, contact the publisher at the above listed address.

U.S. trade bookstores and wholesalers: Please contact
Virginia Archer Publishing
Tel: (1758) 4504159 or email: virginia.archer.poetry@gmail.com

Dedication

To my beautiful and amazing daughter,
who makes me believe in love every day.

Inky Love Sonnet

I'd write you love on paper scented sweet
and add a kiss to words that bear your name,
though rather that I share the glowing heat
of every breath that lights my skin aflame,
than pen you reams of perfect poetry,
for I could never capture you in lines
that do not do you justice, woefully
you stretch beyond this paper, these confines.
So let me write my sonnet on your breath,
as your mouth seizes every single moan,
rewriting words into the very depth
and there within my ribs, reside at home.
The ink, the ink! it fills me to the bone
and writes you there a tale that is our own.

I Still See Your Stars

   I'm not over you,
and I can't promise
that there wouldn't need to be
      galaxies reborn
in my ribs
    before
I stop noticing
your stars.

Deep Carving

You wrote your initials
on my ribs
in cursive flurries,
and grinned
as the tickles
curled my spine
into your hands.

But the curve
of your lips
bent too soon
into wispy smoke,
breathing life
into other flesh,
and leaving me
with this deep carving
of your name
in my chest.

Along Garden Walls

along garden walls
fall shadows advance
a dance

to a tango
of windblown leaves
beneath the mango tree

YOUR LIPS MAKE SONGS MY BUTTERFLIES KNOW

I know
that it would only take
your lips,
brushing the palm
of my hand,
to leave
just a solo note
for my butterflies
to dance to.

SUN SNAPPED HORIZONS

I think that your footsteps got caught
in the prayer of her sleeping breaths,
for they forgot to wander in my direction again,
your shoes, stuck in the lies of your sentences.
Your retreat crept like shadows across rocky hills,
lingering and dark, until your sun snapped horizons
and ushered in my midnight; the stars are so far away
from the swelling moon of my neglected lips.

Lemon Haibun

My hands still smell of the local lemons I was thrilled to grab from a cardboard box in the little supermarket this morning. Pungent aroma of tangy sweetness wafted up from around my wandering feet, as my eyes searched shelves for passionfruit, but found the beckoning gems, skins glistening with fruity oils.

tart smell
lemon oils on skin
fresh perfume

Papered Confessions

My sonnets fall,
confessions
from the remnants
of pressed prayers
between lovers lips,
now
gracing whispered sighs
of pages
caught
between memories.

I breathe you
in paper,
fragile and fleeting.

The Binding Of Stars

They stood apart, like two stars that the dark had defined,
leaving vast spaces unclaimed by breaths,
forgetting that silver moonlight entwined their hands
and the fabric of the very universe wound them close.

Whispered Confessions

She subdued his name
with her teeth
on her questing tongue,
blood quenched
silence
dripping down her chin.

His eyes
stopped
at the guarded gate
of her smile,
drowning in secrecy,
while whispering
her vowels
so softly
on his breath
she never heard
his confessions.

Remembering Curves

Time
is beginning to stretch
the ligaments of my smile
beyond
the cradle of my skull,
and all I desire
on mornings
where the sun struggles
to say a proper salutation
to bones
weary
of not spending the night
curled into your flesh,
is to kiss your lips
and beg your mouth
to remember these curves
before
they slide
from my remaining days.

Spindly Branches

spindly branches
lit by a bright sun
shimmery lake
laps shore

A Sunset Love Affair

When sun has dipped his chin into the sea
and blown his final kiss unto the moon,
the fireflies come dance a reverie
along the fading strings of afternoon,
where orange flares hug tight to purple night
whose eyes begin to open, slow and dark
and bat against the fading of the light
as from horizons, sun, he disembarks.
And as the ocean gives up all its blue
back to the sky and drinks the moony light
I watch within the edges there for you
but somehow you remain so out of sight.
I view the love affair of sun and moon,
a fleeting thing, that ends like ours too soon.

Holding Back Floods

she lets the words
    drip slowly
from the leaky faucet
of her darkest pen
    and mops up
the small splashes
with the corners of her smile

but it doesn't quite reach her eyes,
    or way down in her ribs
where she holds back the flood.

I Tasted Your Words And Couldn't Spit Them Out

Passion
spoke promises from lips
made loose
by fingers
trailing moonlight.

If I had known
that kisses could
cauterize
words
into my tongue,
that would grow
twisted in my ribs,
I wouldn't
have
tasted
you.

Caribbean In November

rainfall
on November leaves
revival
as the dry rustle
becomes green

Is We Culture

Her scolding voice
   rang in the heat of the morning
as the child hiccupped sobs,
and she made no apologies
for shouting her largesse
over the innocent head,
while threatening
   to pick a whip
from the guava tree.

Did her ignorance
   blind her to large swimming brown eyes
and the fact that streams
of warm tears
were further coaxed
by fear,
as small steps
   tried to hurry
along the muddy path
to catch up to her tormentor?

But we will just make the excuse
that this is our heavy handed
Caribbean culture,
not wanting to tangle
with the idiocy
     of the hands
that forcefully formulated
our future.

She Can't Call It Love Anymore

So, is it love that shaped the scars in her smile?
    scooped out with kisses
that meant happiness was formed
only when passion ate its sentences
into her lips?

And is it love
resting ink in her veins?
    waiting for paper
to spill love letters
that no one reads,
to spew hope
foaming like a rabid dog
    on these pages?

I don't know
    if she can call it love anymore -

Hungry Sandpiper

hungry sandpiper
searches sandy shoreline
through wispy waves
for titbits that may have come
as many distant miles as he

Still Dancing In Your Shoes

i

When fear
lay stuck in my throat,
the onus
shouldn't have been yours
to guess
that my hands
shook,
not from desire,
but from
memory.

ii

When kisses
tattooed regret
on the roof of my mouth
I should have stopped
my foggy brain
from rebounding
into your lips.

iii

When I knew
your dance
no longer fit my feet
I said goodbye.

But I didn't let go.

She Left Me With An Open Book

She died as I read my favourite book. I found comfort in the pages of wafting chocolate, as Willy Wonka danced through magical rooms and naughty children were immortalised in rhyme. I remember Easter eggs on the side board, in gaudy purple paper, not realising the symbolism. And I remember the rejection of being forbidden to see her face one last time; adults trying to protect youth from the inevitable. I cannot read that book even now, to the wide open mind of my daughter, without her presence draped over the words. Part of me, all this time later, is still angry at her for not sharing that book with me; but she preferred the kiss of the neck of the nearest bottle, to any press my lips could have plead against her cheek.

rum bottle
emptied without care
unfinished story

White Mist

white mist
on Paix Bouche Hill
anomaly

You Haven't Read Me In A While

My brain pastes angry metaphors of you
along the edges of my tongue,
but my hands have elected
to only carry sorrow to the pages
where your name sits.
Passion has tied my breaths
and forgotten to exhale you
from lungs filled with sooty words
that drift through my ribs,
last remnants of the fire
that once was us.
And surely every garbled message
is written in the ash
for you to simply follow,
but clearly the instructions
are in some foreign language
because you haven't read me in a while.

Bare Branches

branches
reach bare over spaces
denuded
leached pale and worn
by the absence of warmth

Silence Would Be Better Than All These Hollow Words

I measure the words between us now.

Their weight falls
close to tipping every scale
of civility,
that my tongue keeps tied
in knots.

The moon casts halos
along midnight rain clouds,
trying desperately
to be the sun.

I look for excuses
to hear your voice
say anything,
but nothing meaningful
hits me between the ribs,
and yet
my lungs still stutter over emptiness.

The worst conversations
are uttered banalities
that are all that remain
of our collective reality.

I'd rather there be silence.

I Still Long For Summer

Tucked away
in the corners of whispers,
your name
is etched on breaths
that no one else hears.
They cannot see
the flames within my ribs,
and their beliefs
smile prayers into a fantasy
that somedays, I embrace
as mine.

You are sepia snapshots
tattooed on my thighs;
my fingertips
trace
indentations in flesh
made weak with recollection
of June days
and words that we exchanged
in desperation,
now only a litany
recited on rainy days,
when the drum of water on tin roofs
drowns out everything.

But I still long for summer,
even as this December
sits in my bones,
I yearn for your fingers
to clothe my flesh
and make me warm.

I Need To Look Into Your Sun

I watch
as your screens come down
on the fierce sun
you keep hidden behind your pupils,
as you lean in
to plant the tide
along my aching lips.
Somehow, with you
I have to let you know
that I'm not afraid
to be a little burnt.

Bone Folder

I am creased
   and folded
into everything
   you wanted,
your bones
scoring my skin
   with the essence
of your name,
and now
I am a sculpture
sitting cold,
my heart patterned
with the something
we called love.

Poetic Confessionals

I knelt
before your
shifting
seas of thought,
pursing prayers
from lips
knowing only the litany
of your name.

You washed my shores
and back tracked
into rip tides,
pulling me under
until breaths
no longer came.

And we lost ourselves;
now all I have
are poetic confessionals
trying to relieve
bruised knees.

Faded Waltz

Your fingers once wrote a waltz
signed in 3/4 time on my back,
but the music slowly faded
as your voice forgot the lyrics to my name.

Shrill Song

The cockerel shrills his morning song
within the arms of afternoon
while mourning doves, they coo along
the cockerel shrills his morning song
and somehow yet they all belong
although the sun has made leaves swoon,
the cockerel shrills his morning song
within the arms of afternoon.

Paper Butterflies

Your poetry
ran fleeting
through my hands.
Perhaps
I should have
recited
every line,
until I could exhale
each word
you gave
into ink blotches,
making paper butterflies
with your name.

You Drank All My Raindrops

I watch a hummingbird
drinking raindrops
from the shiny edges
of banana leaves,
wings so fast
that it only takes him
a fleeting second
to quench his thirst,
and all I can think
is that your eyelashes
beat
so quickly,
against my cheek
that you trapped
every flutter
in my stomach
and then darted away, fulfilled,
leaving me
breathless
and with this churning
at my core
that won't subside.

Cooler Days

cooler days
coming into bloom
snow-on-the-mountain

Exhaling Your Ink

Teeth
graze the smile
      of curvaceous collarbones
while
      fingers print prayers
into hips
      that only want to obey
the commands
of your hands,
and I
      breathe flustered notes
from my tongue
in the hopes I can remember
the poetry of this moment
and commit
      words to caged pages
where I know
I won't quite capture
how much
      I only exhale
this ink
for you.

Wasp Floating On The Breeze

wasp floating on the breeze
children's squeals

The Illogical Engineer

They say that engineers
are too logical to be poets,
that we are so busy
ensuring
that everything
is so structurally sound,
that we are too enmeshed
in a step by step
of equations
to feel the freedom
of sentences, that cannot draw their own breath
    but someone needs
to send that memo
to my heart,
    cause it missed the fact
that my stomach
    fell out of place from your goodbye
and my ribs have cracked
in a million places
where I didn't reinforce them
against the absence of your smile,
    and I forgot to calculate
the forces of the earthquake
that was you
    on my tears,
so they tumbled down, unchecked
and I don't know
    if I am now so unsound,
that these fissures
can ever be filled with the concreteness
of a love
to make me a patched up semblance of a whole.

The only thing I've learnt
is that words
bleed as often from these hands
as do formulae
and I'm not sure if that makes me a poet
    but
love is the most
illogical constant
that these fingers have ever embraced.

We Never Were A Goddamn Fairy Tale

i

Hollowed out,
   my breaths are stained
   with chloroformed clarity,
where your name
is a tactical forgery
that my brain perpetrates
on my lungs.
I've forgotten
   that folding nostalgia
   into a pocket full of cremated memories
could only tarnish
the coined regret
in my hands.

ii

I cinched my seat-belted pride
as tight as I could,
but my mouth leaked
chain-linked apologies
   that you didn't deserve
   and my lips got stuck
into the curve of sun-burnt smiles
that never quite reached my eyes.
I have been braiding days
  into a rope
  that I will hang from
so that the decadent persuasions
of all the lies
we told each other
will hitch on our dead breaths.

iii

The phantom kisses
that you once laid on my skin
   are etched into bamboo tattoos
   in the crescents of my collarbones,
where the muddy waters
of your former translucent intentions
have clouded my concaved perception
of all that we
ought to have been
   into a fairy story;
   but you aren't a prince
   and I still need rescuing.

You Fill My Every Sense

Your fingers
   taste lips
unzipping moans,
    and the warmth
   of your exhales
smell of summer nights
where we cradled
under a galaxy
   of stars
   that we found
between our breaths.

Charcoal Stained

I drew you
   in ragged breaths
and red lines,
softened your skin
in charcoal outlines
until my fingers
were intimate your profile,
and wrote your name
in fingerprints
   along my ribs.

I am afraid that you have stained
    my hands
and that the only words
left in me are yours.

Walking Barefoot

i

There are too many love poems
about how my feet
are supposed
to know the paths
    away from your unrighteousness,
and how this cloud
that has followed me
will dissipate
    with the sun,
but I haven't found
anything
but rain,
    and these puddles
are thick with mud
    sucking at my feet.

ii

I will leave these tired shoes
at your doorstep
    and walk barefoot in the downpour,
feeling each stone
grind into my soles
    and they will remind me
that I can feel,
that I am alive.

iii

There is no path
where the wind doesn't echo,
      bringing dusty remnants,
but
that doesn't mean
that my eyes won't see
beyond tomorrow's horizons
      even though
you
still cloud
the view.

Reflections In Silver

And as the Moon
trailed her cold fingers
against the midnight tide
she dreamt
about a warmth she had never known,
and that she had only glimpsed
along vanishing red sunsets
that she had been ceaselessly chasing,
little knowing
that the silver
trickling from her fingers
was a reflection
all his.

Thinned Out Love Copies

I think I built you up
    like some legend
covered in stardust,
photocopying
    our love
into a million words

only to realise
    that the copies
are faded replicas
of the actual truth

we aren't supposed
to love each other
anymore.

Unsung Sonnets

He wrote
    scrolled inscriptions
on the curve of my hip
begging interpretations
    of words his tongue
only knew to drip
on skin,
    when
        all I'm sure I needed
was the hushed breath
that held fragile syllables,
    stretched out
on a trembling exhale,
vulnerable
and delicate.

But the sonnets
    tempted by his fingers
stayed gripped
to the roof of his mouth,
    and the lilt of meter
was a song
my lungs
were never taught to sing.

Vibrant Colours

vibrant colours
in a scentless bouquet
wax roses

Radiance

I watch the light
play over his face
as the sun
leans on horizons
and waits for dark.

And all I can think
is how that utter black
will never be too deep
when I can swim
in the radiance of his eyes
until dawn.

I Didn't Have Time To Dance

I felt you
   serenade
my neck with whispers.

I tried to catch
   the quiet words
in a teacup
of moonlight,
   wanting
to sip them slowly,
but clouds
drowned out
midnight sun reflections,
until
the words fell
through cracked floorboards
beneath my undancing feet.

Of Passing Cars And Falling Stars

i

We stood
young under that bright red
     arch
while the rain fell,
and our laughter
swished by with the passing cars
     and was transported
with the step of our synchronized feet,
    arms clasped
and your smile
resting on my head;
    I didn't really need
    an *umbrella*.

ii

Life
lay in the backseat
of that car
   where memories
imprinted fabric,
rubbed in and grimy
   and where
laying on the sandy floor
and muddy from passing footprints,
the red *umbrella*
was left
    forgotten.

iii

The weatherman called for
perpetual rain
      in hurricane swirls
where the last painting
I did of your face
      etched every blue
the sky had graced
on a canvas of yesterdays.
I opened
      the faded tatters
of the laughter we left
in the old red *umbrella*,
   and cried
as the stars fell
one by one.

When Breaking Is A Synonym For Love

She took the last gasp
    of empty air
the room held
    tight
and breathed
a litany of his name
on crests of waves,
    laying bare
every word
she had held
that day
    just for him.

For her
    breaking
was what love
was all about.

Unravelling

He unravelled me,
    with a single
        sweep
    of fingers
to curving
spine.

The Sway Of The Caribbean Woman

She walks along the roadside
    as if her thighs are strangers
and her hips sway
to a calypso
only her breath knows,
    Caribbean woman
embracing the heat
of pavements
    under the slap
of her slipper clad feet
    while her buttocks
roll
  as only
an island woman's can,
and men
  call out "baby"
and "hey gal"
  as she strolls
head high
    in the afternoon sun.

Of Love And Dust

I have carried this I love you on my tongue
for so many days that the words have crumbled
and I'm so afraid that all you will know is dust.

The Last I Love You

Sometimes
   he looks at me
with lost words
on the tip of his tongue,
   and I wait
for the rain of poetry
that never seems to come,
just the tease
of storm clouds
building up
     behind his eyes,
and then the wind
   of the truth
sweeps away
the last
I love you.

A Perfect Canvas

I paint my lips
   in bright red
pretending
that it's all for me,
   but I remember
the smear
along the edge
of your jaw
   as if framed
in that moment;

your skin was the last
   perfect canvas
that I adorned.

Somewhere Between Moons

Somewhere
  between moons
you forgot
that my eyes
had swallowed
  your reflection,
and filled with the stars
you had planted on my tongue
my sentences
became entangled with your name.

  But I didn't see
that your moving lips
    only knew
dead poetry,
  and that love
on your breath
had become
a hollow word unsure of its purpose.

Chasing Sleep On The Nightjar's Call

When the nightjar calls at dusk, as fireflies dance
the arms of the night fold the river into dreamy gurgles
and I chase sleep, as the tree frogs awaken
and I try to lay down the weight of being without you.

With One Glance

There are lifetimes
between our breaths,
and neither of us
has figured out
    how to sever the loop
that spirals us
into nebula,
    but all I know is
we could find each other
in a thousand galaxies
    with one glance.

Breathing For Me

I wondered if he realised
    how every exhale
that got caught
between his lips
    was another breath
stolen,
    and how much
I had begun
to rely on him
to breathe for me.

It seems my gasps got misinterpreted
    as coping,
because he didn't leave
a single drop
of oxygenated love behind.

The Consciousness Of Loving You

So, I get asked whether
   I want to be part of an online programme
where for only $250
self love will spring
from new perception,
   and that I might
finally realise
  that I'm just good enough,
but I have come to accept
that the only consciousness
that my heart understands
   is loving you,
and I don't have to
juggle any other interpretation
of how I'm supposed to feel
   about myself
other than accepting
the depth of the galaxies
   cradled in my ribs
that you put there.

Drinking You In

Savouring you,
   as sonnets trickle
from
   the curve of your lips,
I drink
   love
words.

You Are The Poetry Of My Nightmares

These petrified bones
    got stuck between garbled reflections
of shop windowed truths,
where the sun
    burns skin
    even in the shade,
and where your name
resounds from pavements,
as my feet
    jump gutters
and hurry through a stretch of days
brought to a standstill
by the pounding of computer keys
    that write you
    into my ribs.

I have forgotten
    how to live between sun rise and set,
  where the patterns
  are quilted
  into the ground
through the filtering
of palm frond light
and the buzz of weed eaters,
    and I swear
that I know every damn nuance
of your voice
    and that we have the secret knowing
that we still understand
how to hurt each other
with the smallest words.

Please
    don't come and lie with me tonight,
peeling back white shrouds
from the windows
    of my dreams
and making me feel
the stretch of your warmth along my back,
    while the ceiling fan
twists I love yous
until dawn,
    when the cock's crow
makes a mockery
of my blurred senses;
these bones are almost dust
and I'm too fragile
to withstand your ghost.

Cupid's Accident

We
  were surely accidental,

small breath
of a shared sigh
that the wind blew

    a love
from Cupid's
    hiccup

and the stars
  got crossed.

When The Gleam Left

The gleam
   of your kiss
slowly tarnished
     without me noticing;
you were so busy
eroding our tomorrow,
    peeling pieces
of your smile
in exchange for hers,
   by the time
I understood
your metaphors for love,
all the glitter
had been stripped
from my hands.

Misplaced

You put our love
    somewhere in a pocket
and misplaced it

there has to be a simple
    explanation

tossed in the washing,
    crumpled
pink paper
that we bled on

    because
I can't seem to accept
that we are lost.

Close The Door On Your Way Out

You left,
    I'm sure....

but there
    jammed in the door
of a heart wide open
is your proverbial foot

and I can't shut you out.

Book Burning

His name
sits on the cradle of my tongue,
as the only reference
to love,
and I spit him out
unwittingly
into conversation,
where he haunts
the corners of the room
between sentences.

But if he
is now the thesaurus
for every synonym
to passion,
then it's surely time
I burnt the book.

Believing In Moons

Locked
in our mutual tide
     we orbit each other
on the edge of galaxies,
    where I succumb
to your gravity
and you
   believe in moons.

All I Tasted Was Salt

    Impregnated with
your briny kisses,
my lips
cried you a river
of moans
with words
    ungrasped
in ribs
wanting only breath.

And I drowned
in the churning oceans
    of your hurricane eyes,
and tried to hold on
as you blew me
away.

Catching Silence

Bruised clouds
punch hunkered skylines
with violet promise

I will stand
when the rain comes,
catching
silence
on my tongue.

Of Pillows And Sighs

I woke up today
    with my lips curled around
numbed consonants
and trembling vowels

they tried to say
your name,
    but fumbled
on the edge of my last dream
and stumbled
on the pauses
    of filtered dawn

    and so I let the pillows
catch sighs
and settled into morning.

In Tangles

Our lips
sang shanties,
    threading stars
through fabric, where the very edges
of the universe
clung.

Your song
died to whispers
    in the dark,
and I
am left in tangles.

Somewhere In Between

My tongue is weighted
   by every unuttered sonant;
my brain keeps sending
mixed syllables
and confusing my mouth
with messages
   (*love, hate, somewhere in between*)
until
only the whisper
of breaths through my teeth
     live in the spaces
amid long forgotten moments,
like glitches
mere spasms
and gone.

   It is up to my fingers
to define stars,
but they are lacking
in the dexterity of syntax,
    sinews straining
to spawn nebula
in this endless dark,
     with the limited
vocabulary
of your name.

Folded, Creased And Read

You
have sat on the back of my tongue
for millennia,
    before the stars
grew comfortable
in their constellations
and long before
    my fingers knew
the length of your syllables.

I have caught fragments of you
    in graphite smudges
and black ink swirls
in numbered notebooks,
counting
the times you have come
and gone
    with documented substance
no eyes have adorned.

And it has taken
all these years
    to finally learn
the words to your name
between faces
    that have spawned
the poetry of your truth,
that you are love
    and I never had to give my heart away,
for it was already in your pocket
    folded, creased
and read.

Regret In A Curved Cheek

His cheeks
betrayed the curve
    of his laugh,
brown eyes
a chocolate pool
of forbidden tomorrows
and I knew
    that the song
trapped on his tongue
would find my lips
in future regret

    but his dimpled visage
was too tempting
  and my heart had worn
regret before.

Still Some Stardust

My name
slides off your tongue
as though across
   the sliver of a crescent moon,
slick and fast
as if daylight
were chasing the syllables
   from your throat

and I hold my breath
   convincing myself
that there's still some stardust left.

Bread Thrown

bread thrown
on the neighbour's lawn
chickens squabble

Wearing Daylight

There is a fine line
between the hush of an inhale
and an exhaled scream;

pillows have worn silence
in breaths of night
brought through these curtains
in cold sinks of air,
covered by the incessant banter
of tree frogs

sometimes we get used to the shrouds
of the sheets we bury tears in,
creating ghosts

        but we wear daylight well,
so goddamn well
that you cannot see the cracks
last night sank into.

A Billion Years

You
   are buried
in aspects of my flesh,
like stars
   embedded
in the swirling fabric
of a galaxy;

and I am awaiting
the signs
   of our supernova
to pronounce us dead

but it might take
a billion years.

Love Is Strung And Beaded

Love is strung and beaded
  across galaxies,
far from the clutch of needing hands,
  as cold as stars can freeze.

So why is there a moon dear?
  down deep within my lungs
that craves to breathe your name still
  and bask under your sun.

Fond St. Jacques

The scarred faces of hills
stand in harsh sunlight,
red clay wounds, where fragile soils
grip rock. On rainy days, the land
holds its breath and waits,
hoping that grey skies
won't wash the last hope
into the sea, turned brown
in delta shaped swathes.
Even when the clouds float high
above Mount Gimie, you can still
hear the steady drip from their underbellies
tickled open by the jagged spires
of the mountaintop. And Fond St.Jacques
stands cracked and silent, cradling bones
too deep for flowers to find,
too quiet for prayers to light
on ears that Tomas laid deaf.

Triggering Avalanches

This quiet breath
    lays loosely
between our shoulder blades

   and I fear
that one gasped exhale
could trigger
    an avalanche of words
     wrapped in truth
your ears
  aren't ready for.

Simply Skin

When fingers
   trace pores with highlights
of breath,
skin becomes transformed
  into pathways of stars
under blankets
of moonlight,

but
when the simple act
   of nothingness
is perpetrated
on flesh that once knew galaxies
then skin bereft
   is simply
skin.

Smoke

I let your voice
settle in my ribs

this perpetual cough
that rattles my lungs
with the smoke
of all our yesterdays

still waits...

HALLELUJAHS

You wrote
hallelujahs on my tongue
and left me with songs
too loud for the neighbours,
and a smile
that shouted choruses
at the sun
that the birds echoed
in the palm fronds.
You wrote
your name in my lungs
and your skin
indelible on my palms.
And I wait for you
with bated breath
to see what score
you will teach tonight.

SERENADE

You curved your smile
into my inner thigh
and my heart
rattled every rib
in an effort
to serenade you.

Breeze In My Hair

Your voice
    rings soft like the morning rain
in quiet grey,
and climbs my spine
to intertwine in my hair,
    where the strands
hold onto your breath

    and exhaling,
the clouds of words
    wrap me
in misty watercolours
where the rain
    leaves its tears
in muted lines
along the curve of my lips

and I will taste your syllables
throughout this day
with every swish
    of the breeze in my hair.

Celestial Storm

I'm convinced
    that our hands
have written poetry before;

the stars in my ribs
have known the imprint
      of your lips
for millennia
and your face
      has been a familiar haunting
since I saw the moon reflected there

and even though
our song has been only a murmur
these past years,
      your voice
is still a tidal wave
that drowns butterflies
and floods lungs with ache

for you created
this celestial storm
of poetry
on my tongue.

I Look For You In Every Single Star

I look for you in every single star
that graces inky darkness of the sky
and search for traces of that spark, we are
so broken and I need a reason why.
The nights are filled with dreams of you, I swear
I'm haunted by the whispers of your smile
and I've been blinded by the fading glare
of setting sun, over the ocean's miles.
My bones know only cold, they're brittle now,
my ribs are bowed against my every breath
and I have searched so long I know not how
a love could meet such long and painful death.
The constellations point to all the signs
that you, my heart, you are no longer mine.

The Last Love Poem

If slices of my brain
were analysed
    when I'm gone
I wonder if they would find
the holes
        you
crawled into,
and if the crazy meanderings of all the words
I've been grasping for
    would be uncovered
and the last scraps
of this love poem
could finally be
    written.

Descent Into Poetry

i

We were mismatched pieces of ourselves
    but I always thought
that would make us stronger,
that the jagged edges
would grip tighter
    and we would stay;
instead we knocked
    at each other's corners
grinding away
    until we were more chunks
than we could count
    and you decided
to give some shards away

I'm still here with open hands
waiting for you to grasp
my fingers.

ii

The curve of the yellow crescent moon cupped the sky, and the stars drank. She loved how the cool night air hit her hot cheeks after the stifling heat of the house, that had trapped the day beneath its roof. A goodnight ritual of one last glance at the carpet of the universe before heading to sheets, that she knew would be a tangled mess of dreams before the dawn. She looked at the night sky much more since he left, as if their brokenness could be explained by the constellations, like some crazy pattern she could not quite decipher, but if only she could gather the clues, maybe things could be stitched back together with the poetry of the stars......she never found the answers, but she kept looking anyway.

iii

We loved each other
   until we couldn't call it love anymore;

I have descended into poetry
as a sorry excuse
for these bones to know your name,
   written our epitaph on my tongue
and visit the graveside daily
   with a bouquet of words.

My ink stained fingers
   are a headstone
that show that you are still here,
   a solid rock
in my ribs
and the exhale
on my lips.

I should have just cremated us.

Salvation

The parched ground almost seemed to sigh when the rains finally came. Gurgling gutters rattled down the side of the house and water tap danced on metal rooftop. The roar of sound drowned out the preceding silence, where not even a leaf twitched and the blended green treetops clung to muted birdsong, as if even the birds were too tired for their usual orchestral throes. Grey slowly crept quiet up the hillside and waited, teasing lizards with lingering notes of cool, before the sky opened up and delivered its bounty. I had watched from the verandah as the shadows of the jalousies laid fingers on the ground in the hot afternoon, stirring tea into palatable sips and praying that relief would come. And then it did.

clouds
in a teacup
salvation

Parallel Lines

I curved
my bare lines
into your back
wanting to feel
every molecule,
as if we would blur
into one loved skin;
I forgot
we were parallel.

Back Pocket Of Your Jeans

I searched all over the house that day;

shaken sheets
lay crushed
with ingratitude

your favourite shirt
mocked me
from the chair
where your shoulders had shrugged it

my panicked breaths
left me too,
knocking against my ribs
as they fled

and all the while
my heart
was in the back pocket
of the jeans
you left in.

SMALL THINGS

I do small things;

    when noise permeates cracks
and fills them with busy
the tension eases
for a moment
    and these breaths
ride from ribs
bandaged over
  with the paint
from my sticky fingers,

and I watch the canvas
    drip in shaky lines
and drying memories,
covering blank spots
    with all the blue
these hands have known

and I forget
    that I swallow
round your name, that's been stuck in my throat,
in that last gasp
that wants to perpetually
call you up
call you back
call you here

when I laugh
    and am the loudest at the table
because all I need for an instant
is to hear
anything but you
beating through these veins

but when the small things
collapse in sleep
you crawl into my mouth
      and babble
until dawn
shakes the sheets
and I can swallow you
in small things
again.

Your Fingers Wrote A Sonnet

Your fingers wrote a sonnet on my thighs,
a poem now indelible on skin
that urged from lips the whisper of my sighs
and all the words to cause my head to spin.
You signed your name with flourish at the end,
a cursive wave with heady passion wrought
that made the heat of every kiss ascend
and there within my breaths, each rhyme was caught.
You smiled, then read the syllables aloud
tracing the lines upon my shaking flesh,
almost too much, more than should be allowed
there with command, our words became enmeshed.
Your poetry is writ within my bones,
I carry it with me, never alone.

The Lies I Tell Myself

Your voice
growls into my ear
and blurs
into the butterflies
in the pit
of my stomach;
surely
it must be love.

Hoping For Daylight

Your sun
flashes over other horizons
    and pulls fireflies
in its wake

while I
    watch raindrops course
over occluded panes
and hope
    for daylight.

Where You Left Your Touch

Dead starlight
wakes me
to the stillness of this room,
where
your pillow may lay untouched,
but your handprints
blaze
quiet
from my flesh.

Of Blemishes And Rust

I pick at our memory
    like a blemish,

keeping raw
this melanoma
of thought

maybe I'm hoping
that scars can't form
in cuts left wide open

or maybe I just know
that I will still be licking this wound
    as long as I keep choking
round the rust
of your name
in my throat.

Windy Day

windy day
the sweet lime blooms
make carpets

This Smouldering House

The restless wandering
    of your lips
curls my bones
into slingshots
    and I fire butterflies
    into my mouth
only to swallow them whole again
at the sound of your voice

my ribs
    have become a rattled cage
    where your name lives
and my heart
has crossed borders
into your chest
    and encountered
    a war of sentences
    you have yet to utter

somehow
    this house is smouldering
    and I'm so afraid
    that all we can be is ash.

One Last Sun Splintered Sunrise, One Last Goodbye Kiss

These tremulous years
have shaken the mortar of my bones
and left me splintered,
entwining sunbleached days
into the crevasses of my face

I have seen
sunrises that have wept beauty
and teased me from sleep,
shadows languidly creeping
through an ache of days,
and felt the rain
pit my cheeks with tears

this shattering,
slow at first
has crept in a spiderwork of veins
that has wedged between us,
moss growing
in every nook,
darkened from all our yesterdays,
and I can feel you
pulling away from me
in an agonising rip
that cannot be plastered over
with any words,
for they are all short
of I love you

so I will leave you
with the sandy marrow
of my weakened strength
and lean in
for one last kiss goodbye.

Bereft Of All The Words

The orbital frequency of thought
brings you
from dark sides,
incommunicado,
into the full glare
of first morning cognition
where fingers grapple at sheets
and pray for Saturday's
breath

where limbs are mentally checked
for bruises,
for aches deep set in bones
that have forgotten
what summer hands feel like
on your flesh

what fingers feel like
wrapped in yours,
wefting and weaving
hope
love

and when only air
greets your lips
how coldly the wind is discerned
on your tongue,
bereft of all the words
that say
I need you.

Drunk On Poetry

You were the kind of poet
that didn't need paper,
or keys to caress at 3am
when everything seems too quiet,
except in your head

you had found
the blank paper
pasted over my ribs
and instead
left your words
in bold palm prints
    and fingertip swirls
that sunk in deep
between the interstices
of my breaths

the ink
filtered in kisses
and imparting your name
on my tongue,
like a fine summer wine

I've been drunk
on your poetry for so long,

I forgot you left...

You Don't Taste Like Heaven

What is it
about abject loneliness
that brings your name
like a confessional
to my mouth?

Are you
the only prayer
these lips can form?

Because
you don't taste
like heaven
anymore,
and I'm afraid of this hell
in my ribs.

The Twinkle

the twinkle
just after sunset
dog star

The wave of your breath
hits my skin
    and hitches every inhale
against my shaking ribs,

and imprinted,
 now my every fantasy
is the indent of your smile
along my lips

so close,
    we've become the one word
we're afraid to say
out loud

and all I want
is the brush of your hand
    in my hair
and the touch
of your eyes
on my skin

until I burn

because there should be no space
between
our flames
    while you're turning me into
ash.

The Only Song Left

You are chasing me to say things
you left sitting in my throat;
a thousand proclamations
only pages have accepted as their own

but they are stuck around
every time you quoted
mandarin sunsets into her neck

and no matter how many ways
you no longer care to say sorry,
the platitudes
in each extended sentence
that end in that smile
making the rust boil on my tongue,
the same corrosion
clamping my teeth shut on your name,
I cannot make these breaths
into words
into syllables
that you deserve out loud

and I never wanted us to just be a poem
but these sonnets
are the only song
left.

Perfect Grey

The blood that runs in my veins
doesn't insist on proof of ancestry

or bleed different colours
onto the bathroom tiles

it doesn't care
about the prayers of my parent's differing religions
or the opposing pigments
of their fingers

I am the perfect grey
that they created.

A Single Word

He is October's last hurricane gasp
along my shoulder blades

and I have held this chill
in my bones
since the day
his lips imparted
goodbye into my vocabulary;

it is unfathomable
how much
the exhalation of a single word
can break
a heart.

Your Fingerprints

I haven't come to terms
with the knife
you left in my ribs

I'm still trying to breathe
round the cold blade
of truth

and it doesn't help
that I see you almost every day
like some walking apparition
rising from our ashes

and leaving your fingerprints
on the handle.

Your Smile

Your smile
slits my throat
with every goodbye
those curves have uttered

and I believed.

To That Guy I Met By Chance A Second Time

He has that intensity of stare
that weights time
and makes every dream
you've been grasping at your chest
want to flee your ribs

and he asks if I remember him
and I grant simpering platitudes
that of course I do

I recall the poetry
our lips never read,
but have forgotten
all the words
except
I feel
when I look at him
that he is simply a ghost
that I will never hold

and my arms grow colder
at the thought.

Tango

There's a poem in there somewhere

I don't dance anymore,
I anticipate the pain
that will thread it's arms
through mine and embrace each gasp
with grief

and even in the quiet
of breaths taken between heart beats
I can hear the rasp
of unforgiving fate

but somehow
my heart is still locked
in a tango of limbs
that we created
to some garish beat
that only it knows

and the pain will still be there
tomorrow

there's a poem in there somewhere......

Sunday Prayers

I watch English waters
bubbling like bells
under the draped willows,
and careening into corners
where your name resounds from rocks

even here
where the sun is quiet
you follow with the bees
into cascading beds of colour,
where you mock
my denial

and I say another prayer
into the ringing of Sunday,
where dappled light
dances along the paths of cemeteries
as I try to bury
your ghost

but you were never one
to lie down.

It's Only Spring Cleaning

I will not let these words
sit censored on my tongue

so if you happen to read
how hurricanes have sat
enraged in my chest
or
how the crumbling unquiet
of rain drumming on this roof
have driven my small silences
mad

or if you happen to stumble on sentences
where alliterative allegations
of how much love
I can never again hold,
because it keeps running
through all these cracks you made
between my breaths,
seems to strike you
as a singular neon blink
that is a repetitive flash of your name

get over yourself

I'm allowed to air these musty rugs
in the corners of my own goddamn mind.

Brief Flashes Of Thought

i

Flashes
   dismember darkness
in retinal explosions
that only briefly
   show the real you.

ii

I'm lost
   and stumbling,
grasping at the last image of your smile
as it blazes for a split second
      in the back of my skull,
and I shake headaches
from my mouth
that resemble your name.

iii

You are thunder claps
    in a sky
not quite forgotten.

Never Out Loud

I am at the end of your fingertips
grappling for skin
and I know that you see me
over the edge of this cliff,
with that knowing look
that says
you are waiting until
there are no more other loves
for you to exhaust,
before you reach out
and grasp me back,
like a token you've been juggling in the air,
because my eyes
have always betrayed the way I feel

and I am gasping for the air of your smile
while drowning in every tear
I just can't expunge from my ribs

but my mouth
is quickly become the black hole
where your name has disappeared
and my tongue probes
the rust along my teeth

because I'll never ask out loud...

www.ingramcontent.com/pod-product-compliance
Lightning Source LLC
Chambersburg PA
CBHW021023090426
42738CB00007B/874